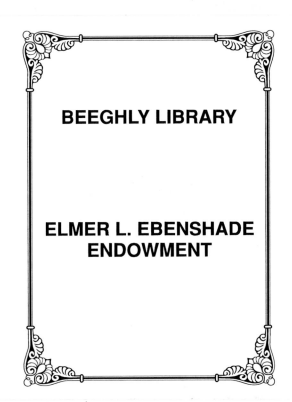

FISHES AND THEIR YOUNG

ALAN MARK FLETCHER

ILLUSTRATED BY
ALLAN EITZEN

PLATY

ADDISON-WESLEY

Addisonian Press titles
by Alan Mark Fletcher

Fishes Dangerous to Man
Fishes That Travel
Fishes That Hide
Fishes and Their Young

 An Addisonian Press Book

Text Copyright © 1974 by Alan Mark Fletcher
Illustrations Copyright © 1974 by Allan Eitzen
All Rights Reserved
Addison-Wesley Publishing Company, Inc.
Reading, Massachusetts 01867
Printed in the United States of America
Second Printing

WZ/WZ   6/75   02053

Library of Congress Cataloging in Publication Data

Fletcher, Alan Mark.
   Fishes and their young.
   SUMMARY: Describes a variety of fish and how they
care for their young.
   ''An Addisonian Press Book.''
   1. Spawning—Juvenile literature.   2. Fishes—
Eggs—Juvenile literature.   3. Parental behavior
in animals—Juvenile literature.   [1. Fishes—Habits
and behavior]   I. Eitzen, Allan, illus.   II. Title.
QL639.2.F58   597'.05'6   73-15619
ISBN 0–201–02053–X

CONTENTS

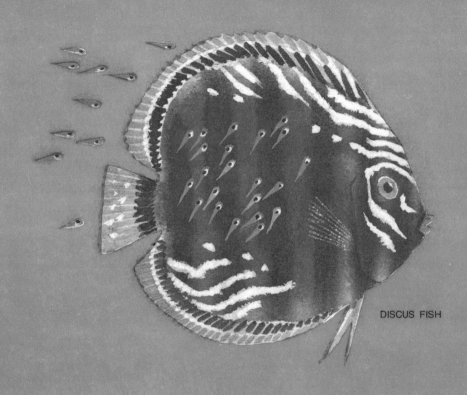

DISCUS FISH

INTRODUCTION

Some kinds of fishes do not take care of their young. However, many kinds do. In this book you'll meet mostly the kinds that do take care of their young.

MOUTHBROODER

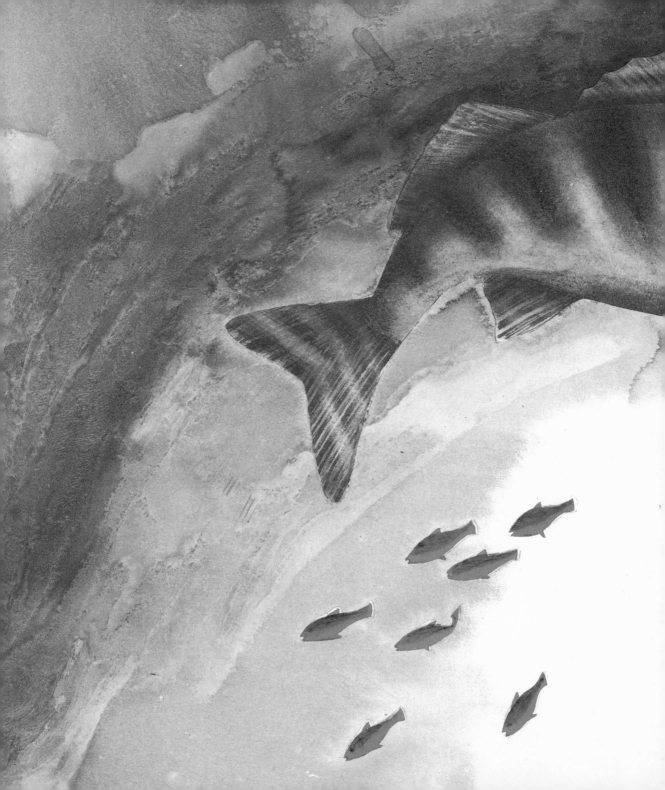

WALLEYED PIKE

CHAPTER ONE

NO CARE
AT ALL

CARP

Carp and Halibut

Many kinds of fishes don't give any care to their young. The female lays the eggs, and with most fishes the male sprays sperm over the eggs. The parents then leave. The eggs are left, and many are eaten by any hungry enemy that passes by. Fishes that do not care for their young usually lay large numbers of eggs. The carp, for example, lays many thousands of eggs. A large halibut deep in the ocean may lay nearly three million eggs. Carp and halibut parents do not guard their eggs, but they lay so many that enough babies hatch so that a few will grow up.

HALIBUT

KISSING FISHES

Kissing Fishes

You may have seen a pair of pink kissing fish in an aquarium. Kissing fish lay a large number of eggs. They float to the surface of the water and drift away, and many of them are eaten by hungry fishes. But because there are so many eggs, a few are sure to drift away to some protected place where the young can hatch and grow up.

CHAPTER TWO
PROTECTED
EGGS

Killifishes

One large family of fishes is called killifishes. The killifishes live over most of the world. Some of them are among the most beautifully colored fishes kept in home aquariums. These fishes give some protection to their young. When killifish lay their eggs, a male and a female swim far in among thick masses of water plants. There they swim among the leaves and roots, laying one egg at a time until 20 or 30 may be laid in a day. Once the eggs are laid, the parents swim off. When the babies hatch, they stand a good chance of living because they are far in among the plants where few enemies can find and eat them.

GRUNION

The Grunion

Along the West Coast of the United States there is a fish called the grunion. Its eggs are laid in sandy beaches when there is a very high spring tide. Thousands of eggs are buried under several inches of wet sand. These eggs are well protected until the next very high tide, usually two weeks later. When the waves once again break over the sand, the baby fish hatch out and are washed into the sea. Once in the sea many baby grunions are eaten by larger fishes. But because a large number of babies hatched, some will escape from enemies.

PLECOSTOMUS

Plecostomus

In the dark streams of tropical South America there is a strange-looking catfish called a Plecostomus. No one has ever watched Plecostomus spawn (lay their eggs). But females have been caught that were carrying a large bunch of eggs under their very big lower lip. Until someone actually watches what happens, we can only guess about the Plecostomus' spawning. We can guess that the female lays her eggs on a stone or on the sand. Then she somehow tucks the large eggs under her lip, where they are safe from enemies until they hatch. Once they hatch, the baby Plecostomus are likely to be on their own. But they are good swimmers right from the moment they hatch, and most of them can swim away from larger fishes.

Lungfish

The lungfish of South America and their cousins in Africa are interesting. They have lungs for breathing air that are similar to the lungs of land animals. When the dry season comes, lungfish are able to curl up in the mud on the pond bottom. There they remain, partially dried out, for several months until the next rainy season. Lungfish care for their young a little more than the other fishes we have read about so far. They dig tunnels in the mud bottom. There the eggs are laid in a nest built of leaves and sticks. For eight days until they hatch, the eggs are guarded by the male lungfish. He fans water above the nest so there is fresh water around the eggs. After they hatch, the young fish live in the nest for 12 more days and the male continues to watch over them. By the time the young lungfish are on their own, they are strong enough to escape from their enemies.

17

LUNGFISH

Sunfish

If you have fished in a lake or pond anywhere in the United States, it is likely that you have caught some sunfish—if your luck was good! There are many kinds of sunfishes, and in different places they have different names. Bluegills, bream and pumpkin seeds are names for sunfishes. All of them protect their eggs.

In the spring the sunfishes dig shallow nests where the water bottom is sandy. The eggs are laid in the nests and are covered over with sand. Both parents stay near the nest and chase away any intruder. To protect their nest they will fight with fishes much larger than themselves.

BLUEGILLS

Salmon

Salmon leave the Atlantic and Pacific Oceans to travel hundreds of miles up rivers and streams to spawn. Because they swim to safer waters, their young have a better chance to live and grow up. Far inland in streams so shallow that there is hardly enough water to cover the parents, salmon bury their eggs in sand and gravel. In the small streams where the young are born, baby salmon are safer. Here, rather than in the

SALMON

ocean, they are not likely to be eaten by larger fishes. The Pacific salmon spawn only once. By the time they have made their long journey and have laid their eggs, they are very tired. Shortly after spawning, they die in the streams where their young will be born. Atlantic salmon return to the sea where they live until the next spawning season. By the time the baby Atlantic and Pacific salmon swim down the streams and rivers to the sea, they are large enough to care for themselves.

Annual Fishes

Another group of killifishes are called annual fishes. We read earlier about killifishes that laid their eggs among water plants. The annual fishes have a very different way of laying their eggs. The South American and African annual fishes live in small ponds in places where there is a long dry season. For several months there is no rainfall at all. Under the hot sun the ponds slowly dry up until there is no water left in them. By the time the ponds are dry, all of the annual fishes have died. But they lay their eggs before they die. Annual fishes bury their eggs in the mud bottoms of the ponds where they live. When the ponds dry up, the parents die, but the eggs remain safe in the mud until the next rainy season. When the rains come, the ponds slowly fill up again, and the babies hatch. The tiny fish grow very rapidly, because they, too, must lay their eggs in the mud before the dry season comes again.

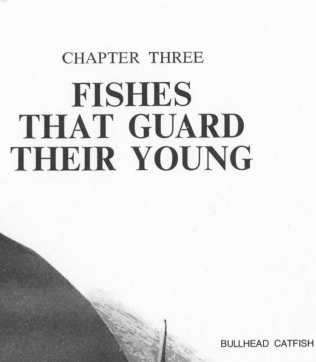

CHAPTER THREE

FISHES
THAT GUARD
THEIR YOUNG

BULLHEAD CATFISH

Bullhead Catfish

Nature lovers who walk along the shores of lakes and ponds in the early summer months are sometimes surprised to find a school of little black tadpole-like fish swimming in the shallow water. When they are left alone the fish spread out among the shoreline plants, but if they are frightened or threatened, they come together in a close group. These little fish are baby bullhead catfish. If you ever see a school of young bullheads, you may be sure that one of the parents is nearby.

Bullheads spawn in a shallow nest on the bottom of the water. When the young bullheads hatch, they form into a school and stay near the parent for protection. At the slightest sign of danger, the babies swim close to the parent because it will fight to defend them. For this reason more young bullheads are likely to grow up than are the babies of fishes that do not give as much care.

BULLHEAD CATFISH

ANGELFISH

Angelfish

In South America, Central America and Africa, there lives a large family of fishes called cichlids. Many kinds of cichlids are seen in home aquariums.

One of the best-known cichlids is the angelfish from South America. Angelfish lay their eggs on flat stones or large leaves. When it is time to spawn, both parents very carefully clean the place for the eggs. Even the smallest speck of dirt is picked up in the fish's mouth and spit out in the water. When the leaf or stone is clean enough, the female lays a neat row of eggs. Row after row of eggs is placed until there are several hundred eggs. The male sprays sperm over them, and then both adult fishes begin moving their fins nearby to keep water moving over the eggs. Any bit of dirt falling on the eggs is quickly removed.

Newly hatched angelfish are at first stuck to the spawning place by a tiny thread. If a baby breaks free, it is picked up by one of the parents and put back with the others. After about two days the babies grow so strong that they continually break free. Finally, putting them back becomes too much of a job, and the young begin to swim near the parents in a school.

Angelfish, however, have a strange way of protecting their young from serious danger. If an enemy refuses to be chased off, the adults sometimes eat their own young.

29

The Discus Fish

Another cichlid, the discus fish, also from South America, cares for its eggs and babies much like the angelfish. But it goes one step further: it feeds the babies.

For years tropical fish breeders tried to raise discus fish in aquariums. It was fairly easy to get the female to lay eggs. When the babies were large enough to care for themselves, the male and female were removed to another aquarium. (Aquarists don't like to leave baby fish with the adults for too long because the adults sometimes eat their own young.) In spite of having plenty of food present, the newly hatched discus fish always died a few at a time. An aquarist who raised ten discus from a spawning of two hundred eggs considered himself to be fortunate.

Then an aquarist in California discovered that if the baby discus fish were left with the adults until they were quite large, most of them lived and grew up. By watching closely, he found out why. The babies pick food from the male's or female's sides. He saw that all of them would pick at the side of one adult for a while. Then after being shaken off, the young would all swim over to the other adult. Scientists have now studied discus fish and have found that they have small food glands on their sides. These glands produce a kind of "milk" that is eaten by the young. Now discus fishes are raised by aquarists all over the world.

Sticklebacks

Living in streams in many parts of North America are pretty little fishes called sticklebacks. There are several kinds of sticklebacks, but they all have the same unusual way of caring for their young.

In the springtime the three-spined stickleback male gets a bright red color on his stomach and digs a shallow hole in the sand. With small sticks and pieces of water plants he builds a nest in the hole. The nest is completely covered over, with entrances at the front and back. Sand is piled over the nest to keep it from floating away. When the nest is finished, the male searches for a female. He dances in front of the female, nips at her and chases her until she swims to the nest. She then swims inside, lays her eggs, and swims out the other side. If other females are near, the male may get several more to lay their eggs in his nest before he begins his work.

Once there are enough eggs, the male will chase away any other fishes that come near the nest, even the mothers. He often blows water into the nest, to make sure fresh water flows around the eggs. They hatch in about four days, and the babies stay in or near the nest for several more days. During that time the male protects the young. Finally the nest breaks apart from much use, and the little sticklebacks swim off to find their own way in the streams.

THREE-SPINED STICKLEBACK

The Siamese Fighting Fish

The Siamese fighting fish, or betta, is a popular tropical aquarium fish. The males have long, flowing fins and come in many beautiful colors. Also the males fight with each other. (Many years ago people used to put them together in small bowls and bet money on which would win the fight.) These fighting fish also have a very interesting way of laying their eggs and caring for their young.

A male fighting fish builds a floating nest of bubbles by taking gulps of air into his mouth and spitting them out. More and more bubbles are made until the nest is several inches wide. The nest may rise a half inch or more above the surface of the water when it is complete. The male fighting fish then chases the female until she swims under the nest. He wraps himself around her, and she drops ten or 20 eggs. As the eggs sink slowly to the bottom, the male picks them up in his mouth and pushes them into the bubble nest. Many more eggs are laid in the same way until the female has none left. Then the male chases the female away, and he alone cares for the nest. While the eggs are getting ready to hatch, the male stays under the nest, adding a few more bubbles from time to time. Any egg that falls out of the nest is promptly tucked back in. The eggs hatch into very tiny fish after two days and then the male becomes very busy. The babies are very wiggly, and as they gain strength they fall from the nest. At first the male picks up each one in his mouth and puts it back in the nest. But within a few days he is surrounded by wiggling, falling babies. They fall out faster than he can put them back. He no longer has time to add new bubbles to the nest as the old ones dry out and burst. At last the male gives up, the babies drift off, and the nest breaks up. And surprisingly, in the end he may eat as many of the babies as he can catch.

(MALE)

(FEMALE)

SIAMESE FIGHTING FISH

COPEINA ARNOLDI

Copeina Arnoldi

A little South American fish called *Copeina arnoldi* has per-haps the most amazing way of caring for its young of any fish in the world. Copeina (pronounced cope-eýe-na) lays its eggs above the water.

In the small jungle streams where this little fish lives there are many leaves and sticks that hang close to the surface of the water. A pair of Copeina ready to lay their eggs swim under a leaf or branch, where they swim around each other very rapidly. Suddenly they swim side by side and jump out of the water onto the leaf or stick. There they hang for a second or two, while a few eggs are laid. Then the fish fall back into the water. Again and again the adults jump out of the water until a hundred or more eggs are laid in a close bunch. Once the female has laid all of her eggs, the male chases her away. Now remember, the eggs have been laid *above* the water, and in the hot jungle air they would soon dry out. But the male splashes water on them with his tail to keep them wet. The male Copeina would attract attention to the eggs if he stayed directly under the eggs. So he stays some distance away. Every few minutes he swims under the nest to splash the eggs with water.

In three days the eggs hatch and the babies sink to the bot-tom of the stream, where they stay until they grow large enough to escape from larger fishes. Copeina will breed in an aquarium if something is placed above the surface. As you can imagine, it is a lot of fun to watch Copeina laying their eggs and caring for their young.

SEAHORSES

CHAPTER FOUR

INSIDE
THE
PARENT

SWORDTAIL (MALE)

SWORDTAIL (FEMALE)

GUPPY (MALE)

GUPPY (FEMALE)

Guppies, Platies, Swordtails, and Mollies

In many kinds of fishes the babies are carried around inside the female. Some of the best-known aquarium fishes give birth to their babies alive and well grown. Guppies, platies, swordtails and mollies carry their eggs around inside the mother until they hatch. This is very good protection. By the time the babies are born they are quite large, and they stand a good chance of getting away from their enemies.

MOLLIE (MALE)

PLATY (FEMALE)

Seahorses

Seahorse eggs hatch inside the parent, but the seahorse and its near relatives do something that no other animals do. Male and female seahorses come together face to face. The female lays her eggs inside a pouch on the *male's* stomach. There the eggs are safe until they hatch. When the young are ready to swim off on their own, the male seahorse hangs onto a water plant by his tail. He twists and squirms and pops the babies out a few at a time.

Mouthbrooders

In Africa there are several kinds of fishes that carry their young around in their mouths. They are called mouthbrooders.

At spawning time male and female mouthbrooders dig a hole in the sand at the bottom of a pond. The female lays her eggs in the hole. Then one of the adults picks the eggs up in its mouth. (In some kinds of mouthbrooders it is the male; in others it is the female.) The eggs hatch after several days, but even after they hatch, the young continue to live in the adult's mouth. Once they have hatched, however, they are spit out from time to time to swim near the parent. If they are threatened by a larger fish, the babies quickly swim back into the parent's mouth. In a couple of weeks the babies grow so large that the adult gives up trying to protect them. Then the young are left to grow up by themselves.

While the mouthbrooder is carrying the babies around in its mouth, the parent eats no food. So by the time the young are ready to leave home, the adult is skinny and weak. Surely the hungry fish must be tempted to eat its own young. And, indeed, sometimes the babies *are* swallowed.

44

The Bitterling

Another fish grows its young inside another animal. The bitterling of Central Europe uses a freshwater clam to care for its young. At spawning time the female bitterling grows an inch-long egg-tube from her stomach. She puts her egg-tube inside the clam and lays some eggs. Several clams are visited in this way, each clam becoming a very safe nursery for the young bitterlings. In a few days the eggs hatch, and the babies stay inside the clam nursery for a few more days while they gain strength. Then they swim out of the clam to begin life on their own. The following year they will be laying their own eggs in a clam, perhaps the same clam in which their mother placed them.

BITTERLING

CONCLUSION

Some fishes care for their young. Others do not. And why this is so scientists aren't sure. What scientists are sure about is that some young of every kind do grow up to have babies of their own. And unless man kills off fishes by polluting the waters, there will be young fishes for thousands of years to come.

DISCUS FISH

INDEX

ABOUT THE AUTHOR

Alan Mark Fletcher's knowledge of his subjects is first-hand: he has made at least ten expeditions into the South American jungle to study fishes and to gather materials for his writings. He spent nine years as editor of *The Aquarium*, a monthly hobby magazine, and has been a senior science editor with two major commercial publishers. A biology graduate of Juniata College, Mr. Fletcher has also taught junior and senior high school science and is the author of seven books, four of them for children. He is now in the Department of Communication Arts at Cornell University. He lives in Ithaca, New York, with his wife and four daughters.

ABOUT THE ARTIST

Allan Eitzen is a graduate of the Philadelphia College of Art and the Minneapolis Institute of Art. Since beginning work as a free-lance illustrator he has specialized in children's books and textbooks. A resident of Barto, Pennsylvania, Mr. Eitzen and his wife Ruth have three girls and two boys.